let's travel in the HOLY LAND

Edited by Darlene Geis

A TRAVEL PRESS BOOK

PICTURE ACKNOWLEDGMENTS
The full-color illustrations in this book were taken in The Holy Land by Ace Williams. Picture 30 is by Brian Brake from Magnum. For the black-and-white photographs we wish to thank George Rodger, Inge Morath and Erich Hartmann from Magnum; A. L. Goodman, Frank Hurley and Sabine Weiss from Rapho-Guillumette; W. Braun from P.I.P.; Orville Goldner; and Photo Researchers, Inc. The map was made by Emerson Barron (Mann Associates).

Original copyright, © 1961 by Columbia Record Club, Inc., New York, N.Y. under the title of *A Colorslide Tour of The Holy Land.* All rights reserved.
New edition published 1965 by CHILDRENS PRESS, INC., Chicago.
Published simultaneously in Canada. Lithographed in the U.S.A.
Library of Congress Catalog Card Number: 65-15976

CONTENTS

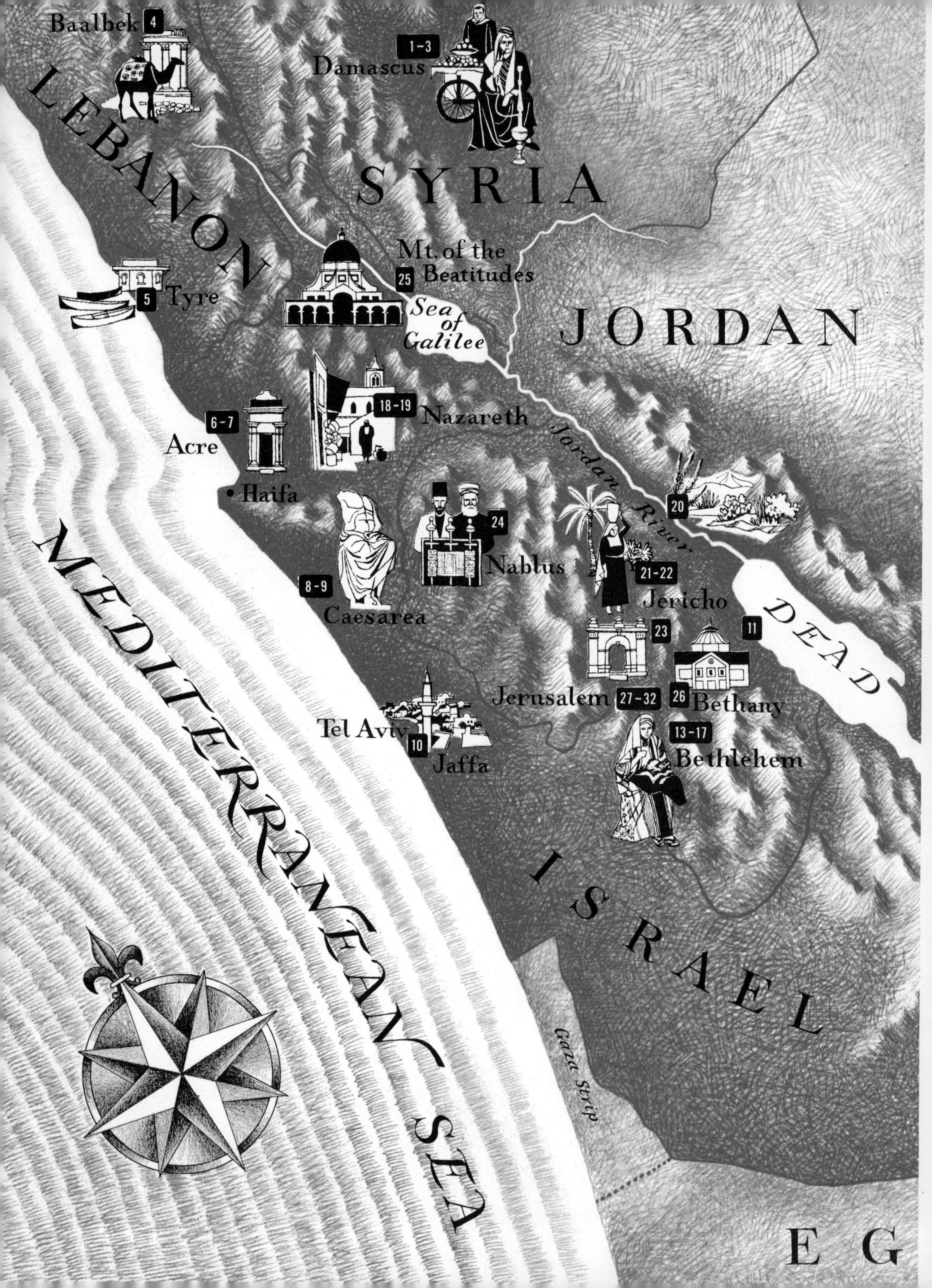
Baalbek 4
1-3
Damascus
LEBANON
SYRIA
Mt. of the
25 Beatitudes
5 Tyre
Sea
of
Galilee
JORDAN
18-19
Nazareth
6-7
Acre
Jordan River
• Haifa
20
24
Nablus
21-22
8-9
Jericho
Caesarea
DEAD
23
11
Jerusalem 27-32
26 Bethany
13-17
Tel Aviv
10
Jaffa
Bethlehem
MEDITERRANEAN SEA
ISRAEL
Gaza Strip
EG

Locales of thirty-two full-page pictures

THE HOLY LAND: WORLD OF THE BIBLE

THE vast sweep of the Old Testament and the New, ranging across deserts and mountains, seems to cover a territory whose horizons are limitless. The still waters, the howling wilderness, far-flung battlefields and cities whose names toll like church bells—all exist in the landscape that every reader of the Bible can visualize, stretching endlessly into the distance. It comes as something of a surprise, then, to visit the Holy Land and find that the Biblical world is in reality very small. It was the ideas born there that reached to the ends of the earth.

Along the short eastern shore of the Mediterranean lies a narrow strip of land that has served, all through recorded time, as the bridge linking the civilizations of Asia, North Africa and Europe. Its history has been a restless one as armies surged across the land first from one direction, then another. The soldiers of Babylon, Assyria, Egypt, Persia, Greece and Rome tramped its sandy soil. And later still, Arab horsemen, Turks and Crusaders battled here. Napoleon, attempting to extend his empire eastward, was defeated on the age-old battleground of Armageddon (*ar-muh-*GEHD'*n*), and in 1918 the British were victorious over the Turks on that same bloody plain.

The value of this small territory was not in the land itself, but in its strategic position as a bridge to richer empires beyond. And the history of the Holy Land is not so significant in terms of wars and conquests as it is in the story of the spiritual developments that took place there and were carried to other countries by returning armies.

Today this war-torn land is sacred to members of three great religions —Judaism, Christianity and Mohammedanism—and it is revered as the birthplace of the Prince of Peace.

PALESTINE, PLACE OF CONTRADICTIONS

The area that encompasses most of the ancient Bible world covers only about 10,000 square miles—little more than the state of Vermont. Formerly known as Palestine, it was divided in 1948 between the new state of Israel and the Hashimite Kingdom of Jordan, and the two nations live side by side now under an uneasy truce. To the north are Lebanon and Syria, parts of which also figured in the Bible stories.

This small area is extraordinary for its geographical contrasts and for the unusual, almost freakish nature of its terrain. Extending along the Mediterranean shore is the narrow coastal plain with its 120-mile stretch of sandy beach overlooking the sparkling sea. Here most of Israel's cities and towns are located, and here the land fulfills its promise with a riotous blooming of spring flowers, fields of corn, fragrant lemon and orange groves, vineyards, fig and olive trees.

In contrast to the fertile plain, the brown Judaean (*joo*-DEE-*un*) hills lie wrinkled and scorched, a desolate wilderness where no blade of grass, no tree, no flower can live. In winter these hills and the mountains to the north are powdered with snow, but the valleys and plains remain warm.

The most dramatic feature of the landscape is the deep Jordan valley, slashing down the country from north to south. The colossal rift in the earth's crust has been, since earliest times, the dividing line between the land of nomads to the east and settled communities west of the Jordan. It was always a great event in the Bible when the river was crossed.

The Jordan rises at the foot of the snowy mountains of Lebanon (LEHB-*uh-non*), flows down into the blue Sea of Galilee whose shores are rimmed with green fields, and then follows a winding course dropping southward to the Dead Sea which lies more than one thousand feet below sea level. South of the Dead Sea the windswept desert of the Negeb (NEHG-*eb*) points like a spearhead down to the Gulf of Aqaba (UH-*kah-buh*) on the Red Sea. Bedouin (BED-*oo-in*) tribes drift across the hot sands, pitching their hairy black tents, their flocks scattered about them. In the middle of the twentieth century, they give us a picturesque glimpse of what the Old Testament patriarchs must have looked like.

It is not surprising that this country, cruel and desolate on the one hand, bounteous and gentle on the other, should have inspired the ancient Israelites with the feeling that God was both punitive and loving.

THE LIVING BIBLE

A visitor to the Holy Land feels a stirring of emotion the minute he sets foot on its historic ground. His eyes lift to the timeless hills, about which the psalmists sang and where the prophets meditated. Atop one of these stony hills sprawls the town of Bethlehem where Christ was born. Another mountaintop is crowned with the Holy City of Jerusalem, its ancient glory shared now by the Star, the Cross and the Crescent. The names of rivers, hills and towns bring the Bible to life, and the centuries fall away as the visitor is carried back to the times of Genesis.

"The desert shall rejoice and blossom as the rose." But farmers toil to make the prophecy come true.

About two thousand years before the birth of Christ, a tribe of nomadic shepherds, much like the Bedouin today, moved from Mesopotamia (*mess-oh-poh-*TAY*-mih-uh*)—which is now Iraq—to the land of Canaan (KAY*-nan*) on the west side of the Jordan. Their leader was Abraham, and the place where he pitched his tents and planted a grove was called Beersheba (*bee-ehr-*SHEE*-buh*), or Seven Wells. Today one of Abraham's wells can still be seen in Beersheba, although the desert town is now a bustling modern manufacturing center, the gateway to the Negeb. It was with Abraham that God first made a covenant, promising him and his descendants "all the land of Canaan, for an everlasting possession" in return for their obedience to Him.

The Israelites' greatest spiritual leader was Moses, who brought them the laws of God and led them back from their bondage in Egypt in the thirteenth century B.C. Three hundred years later the Israelites reached the peak of their national power under three remarkable kings—Saul, David and Solomon. King David built the beautiful walled city of Jerusalem, and Solomon, a splendor-loving monarch of high enterprise, erected the Temple that was to become the glory of the Jews. It was demolished and rebuilt several times before its final destruction by the Romans in 70 A.D.

BIRTHPLACE OF CHRISTIANITY

The country of Judaea had declined to the status of an insignificant Roman province when Jesus was born there. The times were restless, and the hopes of the people were pinned to the coming of a Messiah who, according to their prophets, would restore the kingdom to its ancient glory. The Child who was born in Bethlehem seemed to many to fulfill that prophecy.

We know from the Gospels that Jesus spent His youth in the quiet northern town of Nazareth. The Gospels tell us, too, of His journeyings throughout the small country, teaching, working miracles and bringing to the people of His era an awareness of the deep spiritual relationship between them and their God.

In the years of His ministry, Jesus' travels never took Him more than 130 miles from Jerusalem, and every place of record where He set His foot has been enshrined, first in the memories of His followers, and later by the various sects of the Christian religion. In Jerusalem, particularly, where the events of the Passion and the Resurrection were recorded in great detail, we find a wealth of places intimately associated with Christ's sojourn on earth. This is the very fountainhead of Christianity.

THE EARLIEST PILGRIMS

Pilgrims have been making their way to the Holy Land for more than seventeen hundred years, but strangely enough the earliest ones found less to see there than travelers can see today. The country of Judaea, where Christ had lived and taught and died, rose up against the Romans in 66 A.D. As punishment the Jews were sent into exile, their city of Jerusalem was burned to the ground, and their country's name was changed to Palestine—a word derived from Philistines, the traditional enemies of the Jews.

The first Christian pilgrim to leave a record of his travels came to Jerusalem in 212 A.D. "for the sake of prayer and to obtain knowledge of the Holy Places by enquiry." He found a Roman city rebuilt on the ruins of old Jerusalem. The sacred places mentioned in the Gospels were concealed beneath pagan shrines, but there was a small Christian community living in the city, and its people remembered that under the temple of Venus lay the Holy Sepulcher and the Rock of Calvary.

About a hundred years later, Helena, the aged mother of Emperor Constantine, made a pilgrimage to the Holy Land. Her son had recently built the original St. Peter's in Rome, and he ordered the temple of Venus to be demolished and the Church of the Holy Sepulcher to be erected in its place. In Bethlehem the Grotto of the Nativity was discovered under a Roman temple of Adonis (*uh-*DOH*-niss*), and there, too, a magnificent Christian church rose at the command of Helena and Constantine.

Thus the two great Christian shrines in the Holy Land were established in the fourth century, and from then on, as Christianity grew and spread, pilgrims thronged to Palestine from distant corners of the world.

THE MOSLEM CENTURIES

In 636 A.D. Bedouin tribes from Arabia, united by the new religion of Mohammed, swept into Syria and Palestine, and the long Moslem occupation of the Holy Land began. Mosques supplanted many of the old churches, and on the Holy Rock where Solomon's Temple once stood, the magnificent Dome of the Rock was built. After Mecca and Medina (*muh*-DEE-*nuh*), it is the most sacred Mohammedan place of worship.

Except during the years of the Crusades (from 1096 to 1291) the Crescent of Islam flew over the Holy Land, first when it was under Arab rule and later when it became part of the Ottoman Turkish Empire. During those centuries, Jews who had maintained their traditions and beliefs while living in other lands began to return to Palestine as a result of persecutions in Europe. They found their "land of milk and honey" had become barren and desolate, scarcely able to support them. But it was their spiritual home, the Promised Land, and to the pious, especially, the return to Jerusalem was a shining goal. By the end of the nineteenth century, the Zionist movement to establish a Jewish homeland in Palestine had begun.

DIVIDED LAND

When the Turks lost Palestine in World War I, Britain took over the government of the country under a mandate from the League of Nations. Arab nationalism was on the rise, and it clashed inevitably with the Zionist program of Jewish immigration and settlement in Palestine. In 1948 when the Jewish State of Israel was finally proclaimed, Arab forces made a concerted attack on all the frontiers of the small new country. Its borders were frozen at the time of the 1949 cease-fire agreement, and the Holy Places are now split up between the Arab states and Israel, making Holy Land pilgrimages more difficult than they have been for hundreds of years.

A thorny tangle of barbed wire cuts through Jerusalem, separating Jordan from Israel.

The boundary that divides the Holy Land between Jordan and Israel cuts through the city of Jerusalem, and a no-man's land, scarred with coils of barbed wire and guarded by watchful soldiers of both countries, separates the two halves of the city as effectively as a range of mountains.

The Old City, containing many of the most sacred shrines, lies within

Jordan territory, and visitors usually start their pilgrimage on the Arab side. You are permitted to cross the border only once, so all of the places of interest in Jordan should be seen before going into Israel. In the Old City you will find the Jerusalem of the Gospels—the Golden Gate, marking the spot where Christ entered Jerusalem in triumph, the Garden of Gethsemane (*geth*-SEHM-*uh-nee*), Calvary and the Church of the Holy Sepulcher which contains the tomb of Christ.

The Hashimite Kingdom of Jordan with its Arab population clings to the ancient ways of life, and here one can see the world of the Bible as it used to be. Camel caravans still raise clouds of dust in the shimmering heat of the desert. Women in flowing robes glide gracefully from the village well, balancing jugs of water on their heads. And shepherds continue to watch their flocks on the hills outside of Bethlehem under a starry sky.

In Israel a new nation is growing up on the old land. The tempo and atmosphere are predominantly modern, yet many of the Biblical places retain their timeless magic. The fabled copper mines of King Solomon, awesome reminders of a splendid age, have been rediscovered. The dusty town of Nazareth is white and peaceful still; Mount Tabor (TAY-*ber*), Mount Carmel, the Sea of Galilee and its quiet shores where Jesus preached—all await the visitor with their message from the past.

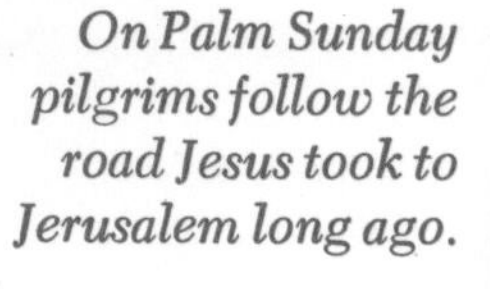

On Palm Sunday pilgrims follow the road Jesus took to Jerusalem long ago.

let's travel in the

HOLY

LAND

BAZAAR IN DAMASCUS: OLDEST INHABITED CITY

ALL the mystery and strangeness of the East color this shadowy bazaar in Damascus (*duh*-MASS-*kus*). Here is a city that was thriving when Abraham first led his family into the land of Canaan. No one knows how old it is, but Damascus is mentioned in the book of Genesis, and people have been living here ever since, making it the oldest inhabited town in the world. East and West have met in this city of minarets and Roman arches, which was governed by France between the two World Wars. Then, with the rest of Syria, she was Egypt's partner in the United Arab Republic until 1963. Today Syria is an independent nation.

Through the arch in this picture passes a street lined with little shops and stalls selling the rugs and brassware, fruit, damask cloth and inlaid wood for which Damascus is famous. This is the old Roman road, known in Biblical times as the Street Called Straight, and it appears in one of the most dramatic New Testament stories.

It was to a little house on this street that Saul of Tarsus was led after he was blinded by a heavenly light on the road to Damascus. Saul had been one of the bitterest enemies of the followers of Jesus, and he was journeying to Damascus to rid the Jewish community there of its members who were disciples of Christ. Instead, blind and shaken by his experience, he was brought to the house of one of the converts where he fasted and prayed for three days. At the end of that time Jesus sent Ananias (*an-uh*-NIGH-*us*) to cure Saul and to baptize him. The man who was to become St. Paul the Apostle, and who would spread the teachings of Christ over the length and breadth of the Roman Empire, was converted and began his ministry here on the Street Called Straight.

CATHEDRAL OF ST. PAUL: SCENE OF SAUL'S ESCAPE

THE rough masonry blocks used in this building were once part of the mighty Roman walls that protected Damascus from desert marauders. Those walls played a part in the story of Saul's sojourn in Damascus, too. After his conversion, the former persecutor of Christ's disciples became an ardent preacher of Jesus' teachings in the synagogues of Damascus. His erstwhile friends, considering him a turncoat, plotted to kill him. Day and night they watched the city gates, foiling his attempts to escape. But the disciples took him one dark night and lowered him from the wall in a basket.

Here we see the massive walls restored and used as the façade of this unusual cathedral, and above the door is the window from which Saul is supposed to have been let down in his dangerous flight from the city. The building, a recent memorial to the ancient Biblical event, does at least give us some feeling of how the old city walls must have looked. And who knows—perhaps these were the very stones scraped by the lowered basket that night, and gripped by the Apostle as he waited to be sure no one had heard him before he hurried off towards Jerusalem and his career as a missionary of Christ.

An artisan in Damascus works on an intricate inlay design—one of the ancient arts of the East.

On the road before the cathedral Arab shepherds are leading their dusty flock in to market from the sandy plain surrounding Damascus. So must they have done through all the centuries of recorded time.

FACE OF THE DESERT: ARAB TRIBESMAN

THE desert nomads have survived for thousands of years in this difficult land, and Bedouin tribes, carrying their tents across the trackless wastes, have outlived splendid civilizations now fallen into ruin. One reason for the Arabs' survival is their changeless way of life, perfectly suited to desert conditions. While other peoples built roads and marble temples, the Arabs' only monuments were wells dug in the burning desert where water means life.

In the towns and cities of the Holy Land we see wanderers like this one. They may have brought their flocks to market or be traveling with a caravan loaded with goods to trade. When an Arab takes his ease, either at home in his tent or abroad in the city, there are two things he enjoys—coffee and tobacco. The coffee is clear, bitter and strong and remarkably thirst-quenching. The tobacco is frequently smoked in an exotic contraption called a narghile (NAHR-*gih-leh*), or water pipe, which bubbles and gurgles cozily while cooling the smoke. The man in our picture is smoking a "hubble-bubble" that must be the granddaddy of all filter-tipped cigarettes.

The Bedouin's costume looks romantic, but it is completely practical. His head is always covered with a square scarf—the *kefiyah* (*keh*-FEE-*yah*)—usually white but sometimes checked in black and white or red and white, and bound with a double coil of black wool or goat's hair. This headdress protects the Bedouin from the brutal rays of the sun and the stinging sand that blows across the desert. The Arab's robes—a long white shirt, a striped silk or cotton coat, belted snugly, and the loose black *aba* (AH-*buh*), or top garment—can be wrapped tightly in cold weather, or allowed to hang loose in the scorching heat. He has worn his flowing robes with comfort for countless generations, and he wears them with pride today. They are the badge of his desert hardihood.

RUINS AT BAALBEK: THE ROMAN PAST

THESE Arab camel drivers and their beasts travel the ancient caravan route between Damascus and Lebanon, passing through the Lebanese city of Baalbek (BAY-*al-beck*) on the way. The camel, with its supercilious sneer, seems unimpressed by the ruins of Roman splendor in the background. Wearing a necklace of blue beads to ward off the "evil eye," the camel walks today where its camel forebears walked, scarcely affected by the march of history.

Caravans trudged through Baalbek thousands of years ago, laden with the riches of the East for Phoenician (*feh*-NEE-*shun*) traders. In those days Baalbck was a Phoenician city where Baal (BAY-*al*), a pagan sun deity, was worshiped. The Greeks renamed the place Heliopolis (*he-lih*-OP-*oh-lis*)—City of the Sun. And the sun blazed down on later caravans carrying goods for the Roman Empire. Two hundred years after Christ was born in a little town about 175 miles south of Baalbek, the Romans erected the Temple of Bacchus (BACK-*us*), god of wine, that we see in this picture, and an even larger Temple of Jupiter. These majestic buildings were included among the wonders of the ancient world, and even now their size and workmanship amaze modern engineers and architects. Earthquakes have toppled great sections of these mighty temples, but enough remains to fill the visitor with awe.

When you stand inside this Temple of Bacchus with its rows of polished columns reaching to the sky, you have some impression of the grandeur and magnificence that must have belonged to the Temple of Solomon at Jerusalem. The stonemasons and architects who built Solomon's Temple were sent from Lebanon as a gift of Hiram, King of Tyre (TIRE), and the beams of the ceiling were hewed from the mighty cedars of Lebanon that grow on the hills just twenty-five miles from Baalbek.

HARBOR OF TYRE: VANISHED GREATNESS

THIS quiet little harbor with its handful of dilapidated fishing boats was once the mightiest seaport of the world. Tyre was founded more than three thousand years ago, and from its calm waters, daring Phoenician sailors voyaged as far as the distant islands of Britain for tin and gold. When Tyre was mistress of the Mediterranean the port was described as "seething with commerce," and it was especially famous for its purple dye, made from thousands of sea snails that were crushed in special mills. Tyrian purple was so highly prized that it became the color of royalty and the badge of wealth and luxury.

Jesus journeyed "into the coasts of Tyre and Sidon (SIGH-*d'n*)," and it was here that He cured a girl who was "grievously vexed with a devil." When Jesus returned to Galilee in His own country, He was followed by throngs of people from Tyre and Sidon who were among the first to flock to His side. They were the multitude whom Jesus fed with the miraculous loaves and fishes because they were without food and far from home.

When the Crusaders came over the seas to wrest the Holy Land from its Moslem conquerors, Tyre became one of the chief cities of the Crusader Kingdom of Jerusalem. But when that kingdom fell, the city of Tyre was crushed, too, its power destroyed for all time. The captains and the kings have departed from this sleepy port, never to return.

The stately cedars of Lebanon tower like cathedral arches high on a mountain slope.

RAMPARTS AT ACRE: CRUSADERS' STRONGHOLD

ALONG the Mediterranean shore of Lebanon and Israel the old coastal towns keep their crumbling mementoes of the Crusaders. Tyre and Sidon have moldering sea walls that were built for the defense of their harbors. And on many a hill overlooking the Mediterranean, medieval castles still stand, like a mirage of Europe seen in the golden heat of this Eastern land.

Here in Acre (AH-*k'r*), a seaport on the northern coast of Israel, the rough Crusader stones bring back memories of Richard the Lionhearted, who captured this city from its Moslem leader Saladin (SAL-*uh-din*) in 1191. A hundred years before, the knights of the First Crusade had successfully taken much of the Holy Land and established a Christian Kingdom of Jerusalem. This was won back from them by the Moslems, united under Saladin, and though King Richard was able to recapture Acre, the Holy City of Jerusalem remained in Moslem hands until World War I.

Saladin explained to Richard, "Jerusalem is as much to us Mohammedans as it can be to you Christians, and more. It is the place where our Prophet made his night ascent to heaven, and it will be the gathering place of our nation at the Great Judgment." At Acre today, the ramparts and watchtower rebuilt from the walls of Christian knights overlook a white Moslem mosque, in a city that belongs to Israel.

The Krak des Chevaliers, a Crusader citadel, broods above the Syrian plains.

MOSLEM MINARET: CALL TO PRAYER

THE prayers of many faiths are offered up in the Holy Land where the pealing of Christian church bells mingles with the cry of the muezzin (*mew*-EZ-*in*). These are the sounds that herald each day's dawning, for as soon as the sun rises, convent and monastery bells ring for matins (MAT-*ins*)—the morning prayers—and high on his little balcony the muezzin chants, "*Allâhu akbar, Allâhu akbar* . . . Allah is great; testify that there is no God but Allah and Mohammed is his Prophet. . . . Come to prayer!"

Five times each day the reverent Moslems kneel to pray, with forehead touching the ground, and facing toward Mecca, the Arabian city where Mohammed was born. They must also acknowledge God, with Mohammed as his Prophet; they have to help the poor; fast from sunrise to sunset during the days of Ramadan, their ninth month; and if possible every Moslem must make a pilgrimage to Mecca.

The religion of the Moslems was formulated by Mohammed, who claimed divine revelations from God, in the form of the Koran (*koh*-RAHN), a holy book. In the seventh century when Mohammed lived, Arab paganism had already been somewhat influenced by Judaism and Christianity, and the Prophet himself said that his revelation agreed with Jewish and Christian scripture. But Mohammed was a military leader as well as a prophet, and those who fought on his side were forced to embrace his religion. His vanquished enemies had the choice of death, conversion to Islam or payment of tribute. The Moslem's zealous faith has played a large part in unifying the eighty million people of the Arab world.

The muezzin's singsong cry has become part of the Holy Land, and the creed of Islam, set forth in the Koran, takes its place beside Christianity and Judaism there: "We believe in God, and the revelation given to us and to Abraham . . . Moses and Jesus, and that given to [all] Prophets from their Lord: we make no difference between one and another of them: and we bow to God . . . [in Islam]."

STATUE AT CAESAREA: HEROD'S CITY

THE Holy Land is a treasure-trove of many civilizations, and here in the ruins of Caesarea (*see-zuh-*REE*-uh*) we see the ghost of a once-splendid Roman seaport built by Herod the Great. This wily ruler of Judaea named the city in honor of Augustus Caesar, his imperial patron, and the flattering gesture undoubtedly helped his cause in Rome.

Herod's city was enclosed within a curving wall three miles long, and it faced a harbor that was a miracle of engineering for those times. The city was dazzlingly modern, its streets laid out symmetrically, its buildings rising in marble splendor with theaters, a forum, a palace, a temple, and a hippodrome that could seat twenty thousand spectators. Caesarea was a little bit of Rome transplanted in all its elegance to the rougher, less polished colony of Judaea.

The old harsh city of Jerusalem high on its hill remained the capital of the Jews, but the Roman governors of Judaea preferred to live in more civilized Caesarea. Out of deference to the Jewish laws against the likeness of any living thing, there were no statues decorating the buildings in Jerusalem. But in Roman Caesarea, stone figures of the Emperors in their draped robes ornamented halls and courtyards.

In Jesus' lifetime Pontius Pilate, who was the governor of Judaea, lived in Caesarea. It was from this gleaming city that he and his court went up to Jerusalem for the Passover holiday at which Pilate condemned Jesus to the cross.

Today a road bordered by broken columns leads to the ruins of Herod's city. Members of a nearby kibbutz (*kee-*BOOTS), or communal farm, came upon the statue in this picture when they were clearing stones from a field, and now archaeologists are excavating the site in hopes of reconstructing one of Israel's historic cities.

MEDIEVAL CAESAREA: CRUSADERS' WALL

THE mark of the Crusaders is found in Caesarea, too. Herod's fine seaport had dwindled in importance during the time the Arabs held the Holy Land. But when the Crusaders were forging their chain of coastal cities they appreciated the value of the harbor with its long breakwaters. Baldwin I, the first King of Jerusalem, took the city in 1101 and put its inhabitants to death by the sword.

A small section of the old city, well within Herod's Roman walls, was fortified by the knights to serve as a citadel guarding the harbor. You can see the powerful wall in the background, and over what used to be a moat, three stone arches still stand. The bridge that they supported once rang to the hoofbeats of horses and the clatter of armored knights as they rode forth to battle the infidels. Many of the Crusaders must have learned to their sorrow that the climate of this palmy land was not ideal for steel suits. But just as earlier Romans brought Rome to these shores, the Crusaders carried their European ways with them. They also carried back to Europe fabulous booty from the Holy Land. In Caesarea, King Baldwin found one of the great treasures of the Crusades—an ancient green crystal vase believed to be the Holy Grail, the chalice used at the Last Supper.

Crusaders, inspired with holy zeal, captured Jerusalem from the infidels and raised the banners of Christendom there.

VIEW FROM JAFFA: OVERLOOKING TEL AVIV

SOME of the stone blocks from the ruins of Caesarea were brought here to Jaffa (JAF-*fuh*) in the nineteenth century to be used as building materials. Though they would seem ancient to us, they were relatively new additions to this city whose beginnings are said to go back to the Flood when Japheth (JAY-*feth*), the son of Noah, founded it. The old city stands on a small hill jutting out into the blue Mediterranean, and beyond its bay the young and vigorous metropolis of Tel Aviv (TEL *ah*-VEEV) has sprung up in just the past fifty years.

Old Jaffa and new Tel Aviv have merged now, the one steeped in the history of the Bible, the other actively engaged in creating the modern history of Israel. Although Jerusalem is the capital of Israel, Tel Aviv-Jaffa with a population of 430,000 is its largest city, whose new citizens have poured into it from seventy-two different lands. In Tel Aviv you will find "foreign sections" that reflect the varied backgrounds of the people —Yemenite (YEHM-*en-ite*), Russian, Lithuanian, Polish, German, Austrian, Central European—for this is a melting-pot community not unlike other large cosmopolitan cities. The similarity goes even further for Tel Aviv is a big industrial center, and its energy and activity are not characteristic of the Middle East's slower tempo.

Jaffa, surrounded by orange groves and orchards, belongs to another world. Turn away from Tel Aviv and look out to sea instead. This is the port (called Joppa in those days) from which Jonah set sail for Tarshish and was swallowed by a whale. Into this harbor the ships of King Hiram of Tyre sailed, loaded with the fragrant cedar timber for Solomon's Temple. And it was Jaffa, younger then and a bright jewel against the blue sea, that Mark Antony gave to Cleopatra as a token of his affection.

BESIDE THE STILL WATERS: THE DEAD SEA

MOTIONLESS and smooth, the mineral-laden waters of the Dead Sea mirror mountains, sky and people. A sense of mystery hangs over this place, perhaps because the lifeless shores are so hushed. Nothing lives in the briny water of the Dead Sea or on its salty banks, and there is no splash of fish, no whispering of grasses or trees to break the silence. A smell of sulphur and chemicals hangs in the quiet air, giving rise to the story that birds cannot fly here because the fumes are poisonous, though scarcity of food is probably the real reason.

Lying at the lowest part of the Jordan Valley, 1290 feet below sea level, the Dead Sea is 1200 feet deep. The Jordan River pours nearly seven million tons of water into it daily, but since the Dead Sea has no outlet, and evaporation takes place very quickly in the heat, its water is left with an enormous residue of chemicals and salt. This wealth of minerals and chemicals is just being developed, and factories and refineries are springing up in the desolate hills.

In 1947 an Arab herdsman was searching for one of his goats up in the lonely cliffs at the northwest end of the Dead Sea. There he stumbled upon a small cave in the rocks, and hidden in the darkness he found a number of earthenware jars containing scrolls. The Dead Sea Scrolls turned out to be the oldest Biblical manuscripts in existence, lost for two thousand years on these silent shores. Their discovery is one of the archaeological sensations of the twentieth century.

The Dead Sea Scrolls, which cast new light upon the Bible, were found in this dark cave.

KING SOLOMON'S MINES: HILLS OF COPPER

THE archaeologists' spades have been busy in the Holy Land, turning back time as they turn back layers of earth and revealing to us the fabled places of the Bible. For the Book is closely bound up with the land, and in World War I the British General Allenby found the Bible one of his most reliable sources of information about water, strategic sites and natural strongholds. Although the Bible is primarily concerned with theology, recent explorations are proving its accuracy as a historical record, too.

Copper and iron had never been found in Palestine in recent centuries, although the Bible had described the Promised Land as a place "whose stones contain iron and in whose hills you can mine copper." About twenty-five years ago archaeologists, taking their clues from the Bible, found a series of copper-mining ruins in the desert wastelands of the Negeb. Near the Gulf of Aqaba they also found the remains of Solomon's Red Sea port from which his ships sailed to Arabia to trade iron and copper for spices, incense and gold from the Queen of Sheba's country. Here we see the towering cliffs of copper-bearing sandstone at one of Solomon's mining sites. Traces of miners' living quarters and smelting ovens have been found here, and the Bible tells us that at one time 80,000 people worked the royal mines that produced the wealth which Solomon lavished on his proud city of Jerusalem.

Bedouin women on the streets of Beersheba move with a jingling of silver coins.

WOMAN OF BETHLEHEM: DRESS OF MANY COLORS

THE Song of Solomon takes on new meaning when we see a woman of the Holy Land dressed in the colorful Bethlehem costume. "Behold thou art fair, my love, behold thou art fair . . . thy cheeks are comely with rows of jewels, thy neck with chains of gold." The gold coins worn around this girl's veil are her dowry, and when she marries she will wear, under the veil, a high-pointed fez with her coins sewed to it. Some say this head-dress was borrowed from the Crusaders' ladies who wore tall pointed caps under gauzy scarves, and others believe that the medieval fashion was brought back to Europe from Bethlehem by French ladies who were style-conscious even on Crusade.

This Bethlehem girl, diligently embroidering a magnificent costume, reminds us of another Bible heroine—Ruth, who came from her own land to Bethlehem as a faithful daughter-in-law. "Whither thou goest, I will go," she told Naomi, and far from her own people she gleaned corn in the fields around the city. Ruth's great-grandson was the shepherd boy of Bethlehem who became king of Israel. In these stony fields young David tended his father's flocks, learned to use a slingshot with deadly skill, and played sweet songs upon his harp.

A thousand years after David's time, the Romans ruled this land, and Caesar Augustus decreed that everyone was to be taxed, each in his own city. That was why Joseph brought Mary from Nazareth to Bethlehem, the city of David, "because he was of the house and lineage of David." And so it happened that Bethlehem became the birthplace of Jesus, fulfilling Micah's prophecy: "But thou, Bethlehem, though thou be little among the thousands of Judah, yet out of thee shall come forth [Him] that is to be ruler in Israel."

LITTLE TOWN OF BETHLEHEM: CITY OF CHRISTMAS

OF ALL the Bible cities Bethlehem is the one that most stirs our imagination. People in northern lands have pictured steep-roofed houses clustered on a hill, snugly blanketed with snow and gleaming in the frosty light of the December stars. And the colors of Christmas in the north are the bright green and red of holly, the white sparkle of snowflakes. How different the real Bethlehem is!

Here we see its flat-roofed buildings bleached bone-white by the dazzling sun. Bethlehem is built on the terraced slopes of two hills, and its narrow streets are sandy and treeless, almost devoid of color. Rising like slim sentinels above the city are the pale bell towers of numerous monasteries and convents, and the ringing of their bells is the special music of Bethlehem. Under the hot skies, chime answers chime as though the Christmas tidings were ringing out each day.

Bethlehem has always been a market town, with fields of wheat (called "corn" in the Bible) spread out below it. Its name means "House of Bread," and its bake shops still make the round flat loaves used in Bible times. But ever since the first Christmas star guided shepherds and wise men to the manger where the Christ Child lay, pilgrims have been making their way to Bethlehem. Some of the Crusaders lingered here, and today many Christian Arab families of Bethlehem show evidence of European ancestry in their blue eyes, fair skin and pink cheeks.

The Bethlehemites are skilled craftsmen, and the little shops lining their streets sell rosaries, pearly shell crucifixes and olivewood covers for Bibles—all products that are made here to be sold to pilgrims. As you walk the narrow streets of Bethlehem you can see the artisans at work in their little shops and hear them singing their wailing Arab tunes—an odd sound in a city associated in our minds with Christmas carols.

FIELD OF THE SHEPHERDS: WATCHING THE FLOCKS

IN THE arid hills outside of Bethlehem, scenes like this echo the story of the first Christmas: "And there were in the same country shepherds abiding in the field, keeping watch over their flock by night." As the shadows lengthen, the plaintive music of the shepherd's reed sounds over the quiet field. The flocks will gather, and the men will prepare to keep their vigil under the darkening sky. Later, when the stars come out, the shepherds will take turns sleeping and guarding the sheep, using the movements of the stars to time their watch periods. Any strange sound seems menacing in the silent night—the call of a wild animal or the clatter of a stone rolling downhill makes the sheep stir restlessly and puts the shepherds on the alert. When we see these men in their lonely empty land, the Christmas story unfolds again in more vivid detail.

This is how it must have been when the shepherds of that First Christmas saw the angel "and the glory of the Lord shone round about them: and they were sore afraid." We can imagine simple shepherds like these filled with wonder as they talked among themselves about the angel's "tidings of great joy," and we can almost see them getting to their feet, shaking out the folds of their robes, calling to their sheep and hurrying up the rocky slopes to Bethlehem in order to "see this thing which is come to pass which the Lord hath made known to us."

Like the wise men of old, these Bedouins use camels to carry them through the Holy Land.

CHURCH OF THE NATIVITY: OLDEST IN THE CHRISTIAN WORLD

WHEN the shepherds and the wise men from the East came to Bethlehem they found the Christ Child lying in a manger in a small cave. There, under the bright Christmas star, a scene of touching intimacy took place as the travelers gathered about the Holy Family to worship the newborn Infant. That little grotto is enshrined now within the massive walls of the Church of the Nativity, the most ancient Christian church in use today.

Emperor Constantine built the present basilica in 325 A.D. and, unlike other churches in the Holy Land, this one has come down through the centuries unharmed by destructive invaders. When the Persians swept through Palestine in the seventh century they destroyed the Holy Sepulcher and many other churches, but spared the Church of the Nativity when they saw a mosaic depicting the wise men, or Magi (MAY-*jigh*), in Persian costume. Later, Moslems found that the western apse of the church faced Mecca, so for hundreds of years they used the church as their own place of worship, even making special pilgrimages to Bethlehem. The entrance to the church is low and narrow, a tiny opening left within a larger blocked-up doorway, which you can see in the far wall. It is barely large enough for one person to pass through bending very low, and they will tell you in Bethlehem that all the other doors were walled up centuries ago to keep mounted Moslems from riding their horses into the church.

Once you have passed through the narrow door you find yourself in the immense Roman basilica of Constantine. The very air is heavy with antiquity, and in the murky light you see the austere grandeur of massive Roman columns, and the faded patches of old gold Byzantine mosaics. But all this is still not what you came to see. Beneath the high altar is a chamber, part cave and part masonry—the grotto where Jesus was born.

GROTTO OF THE NATIVITY: WHERE CHRIST WAS BORN

A DARK little staircase leads down to the Grotto of the Nativity. Here in the flickering light of candles and the glow of silver oil lamps is a small cave, its blackened walls hung with rich fabrics and tapestries. A marble slab on the floor holds the silver Star of Bethlehem, marking the traditional site of the Nativity. The inscription around the star has been nearly worn away by pilgrims' kisses, but you can still read in Latin, "Here Jesus Christ Was Born of the Virgin Mary." This dark cave, smelling of incense, seems most unlike our accustomed picture of a wooden stable, a manger filled with golden hay, and the warm steamy smell of farm animals.

Bethlehem still has houses built over caves like this one, and many of them go back to the time of Christ. The caves are at ground level, and they are used to stable the animals, while the family lives in a chamber above, reached by a flight of stairs. When Mary and Joseph were unable to find room at the inn, they may well have been taken in by a hospitable Bethlehem family who offered them their downstairs cave. Church tradition says that Jesus was born in a cave rather than an inn or stable, and this grotto with its manger hewn out of stone has been venerated as Christ's birthplace since the first century A.D. Nevertheless, visitors to the Holy Land are sometimes surprised to find the reality so different from their cherished imagining.

Christmas Eve in Bethlehem brings a reverent procession to the Church of the Nativity.

STREET IN NAZARETH: COUNTRY VILLAGE

THIS is the town where Jesus spent the years of His childhood and where He grew to manhood. Nazareth was an unimportant village in those days, cupped in a valley and built in terraces against the surrounding hills which protect and shelter it from the outside world. Nazareth means "the guardian," and this remote town in northern Galilee was the custodian of those years in Jesus' life about which so little is known. We know that Joseph was a carpenter and that Jesus may have assisted him. Today there are carpenters in Nazareth who still work in the age-old manner. Their little shops are open to the street, and the aromatic smell of fresh wood shavings drifts out of doors. The carpenter sits on the floor using primitive tools, surrounded with piles of old-fashioned plows, yokes and threshing boards.

The narrow hilly streets, with gutters in the middle, wind between rows of Arab shops in this, the largest Arab town in Israel. And here we see a street that Jesus Himself may have walked. For the old synagogue where He went to school stands within the Greek Catholic church in the background. The Gospel of St. Luke tells us that it was here that "The Child grew, and waxed strong in spirit, filled with wisdom: and the grace of God was upon Him." In the synagogue at Nazareth, Jesus observed sadly to His unbelieving townsmen, "No prophet is accepted in his own country."

The old and humble trades take on a special dignity in Nazareth, where a Carpenter once lived.

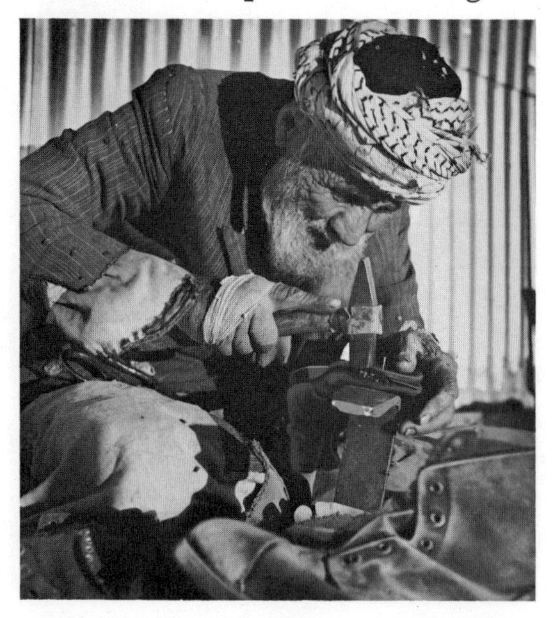

THE VIRGIN'S SPRING: VILLAGE FOUNTAIN

PILGRIMS and tourists come to Nazareth today not only because it was the boyhood home of Jesus, but because it was here that the angel Gabriel announced the birth of Christ to the Virgin Mary. The Church of the Annunciation is built around the grotto which was part of Mary's house, and Franciscan monks have tended the sacred site for centuries. But it is the Virgin's Spring, pictured here, that most nearly captures the essence of ancient Nazareth.

There is only one well in all the town and its water gushes cold and pure from this fountain. Here the village women have been gathering through all the years of Nazareth's history, gossiping and then moving off with full jugs balanced on their heads. The women of the Holy Land have an extraordinary grace and queenly bearing as a result of carrying jars and other heavy objects in this manner, and when we see them, we seem to see the women of the Bible—Rebecca, Esther, Mary—moving with stately dignity about their modest tasks. Surely Mary herself must often have come to this very fountain to draw water for her family, and it is possible that many times she was accompanied by her little Child.

Throughout the Holy Land, fountains, springs and wells are cherished. During the hot and rainless months of the year, this country without forests becomes parched and barren, and its sources of water are the sources of life. Around a village fountain like this the delicious music of splashing water, the refreshing coolness of wet ground instead of sun-bleached sand, is a feast for the senses. The authors of the Bible, knowing their land so well, wrote feelingly about the preciousness of water and the agony of thirst.

THE JORDAN: HALLOWED RIVER

WE HAVE sung about the Jordan in hymns and spirituals, for this is the river that flows through the Holy Land and runs through many of the books of the Bible as well. Joshua led the Israelites across the flood-swollen river and into the Promised Land, lepers are said to have been cured after bathing in its muddy water, and it was here that John the Baptist brought his followers to be baptized and confess their sins.

Again, the actual Holy Land site does not quite match our image of it. At first this winding river between its muddy banks seems disappointingly small and ugly. Considering the great events that took place here, we would expect to see a mighty river coursing through a countryside of imposing grandeur. But standing on these reedy banks, where the silence is broken only by the song of birds, we realize that the world of the Bible was a small and intimate place and its grandeur lies in its simplicity.

Tradition says that at this very bend in the river Christ was baptized by John the Baptist. Here the valley lies more than a thousand feet below sea level and is only five miles from the Dead Sea. The lush vegetation of the upper valley has given way to the desolation of the wilderness, where the heat has a leaden oppressiveness. In the distance, naked hills roll toward the horizon, while the thickets are alive with vipers, wild boars, jackals, scorpions and small panthers. This is the wilderness where John the Baptist preached, clothed in camel's hair and wearing "a girdle of skin about his loins," living on locusts and wild honey. In such a bleak and lonely spot, wasted and terrible, the lessons of repentance and faith could be taught most strikingly.

For centuries pilgrims belonging to the Russian and Greek Orthodox churches came each year to this stretch of the river to commemorate Christ's baptism. As many as sixty thousand at a time, dressed in white shrouds and carrying lighted candles, would walk into the Jordan waters at dusk. The voice crying in the wilderness had carried to distant lands.

MOUNT OF THE TEMPTATION: VIEW OVER JERICHO

AFTER Jesus was baptized in the Jordan He was led into the wilderness to the top of a mountain where He fasted for forty days and forty nights and was tempted by the Devil. Here, rising behind the oasis of Jericho, is the mountain of Christ's temptation, and this is the sweeping panorama of valley and the mountains of Moab (MOH-*ab*) that He must have seen. "All these things will I give thee," said the Devil, "if thou wilt fall down and worship me." But Jesus answered, "Get thee hence, Satan: for it is written, thou shalt worship the Lord thy God, and Him only shalt thou serve." And so the forty-day ordeal was passed, and the Tempter was vanquished. Jesus went down from the mountain to begin His ministry in Galilee, and the Gospel of St. Matthew tells us, "From that time Jesus began to preach."

Nineteen hundred years have brought few changes here, and visitors who climb the steep zigzag path to the summit of this rocky hill can see the Bible land spread out below, much as it was in the time of Christ. Halfway up the mountain the Greek Monastery of the Forty Days clings to the edge of the cliff. The dozen or so monks who live here are friendly and hospitable to any visitors at their gate, and gladly show them through the monastery and offer them refreshment. It is an ancient courtesy to treat a stranger as if he might be Christ wandering again on earth, and here where He fasted the stranger is fed.

Arab refugees near the Mount of the Temptation wait for food and supplies with fatalistic patience.

FRUITFUL JERICHO: OASIS IN THE WILDERNESS

THE fertile green fields, gardens and fruit groves of Jericho are a startling contrast to the bone-dry landscape that surrounds them. And the secret of this flowering in the wilderness is water—Elisha's (*ee*-LIGH-*shuhs*) Fountain, which gushes a thousand gallons of sweet spring water a minute to nourish the land around it. Thanks to this plentiful spring there have been many Jerichos in the course of history. Archaeologists have been amazed to discover that there was a walled community here as long ago as 5000 B.C., making it the earliest known settlement in the world. On top of its remains there are the ruins of at least sixteen later communities.

The Jericho of 1200 B.C. was the one whose walls tumbled before Joshua's trumpets. But no matter how often the city was destroyed, settlers always came back to this place beside Elisha's Fountain where the desert could be made to bloom. This exotic garden where dates, balsam, fruits and grain grow among the palm trees was another of Mark Antony's gifts to Cleopatra, and the Egyptian queen came here to Jericho about 35 B.C. to inspect her property. Ever the shrewd businesswoman, Cleopatra took a shoot of balsam with her to start a grove in Egypt, and then she rented the Jericho balsam groves to Herod for the equivalent of one hundred fifty thousand dollars a year.

Today, Old Testament Jericho is just a mound of sandy earth and stone. In its debris of centuries of civilization, archaeologists mine the precious bits and pieces of history. On one side of the mound is the lush garden town of present-day Jericho, a village of about a thousand Jordan Arabs, many of whom are descendants of the Negroes who once were slaves of the Arabs. On the other side of the mound is a dreary, sun-baked community of Arab refugees from Israel. They are huddled in mud huts, homeless wanderers who have settled near the life-giving waters of Elisha's Fountain until the Arab-Israel issue is settled.

THE INN OF THE GOOD SAMARITAN: ANCIENT CARAVANSERAI

THE road that winds down from the heights of Jerusalem to Jericho in the Jordan valley is an old caravan route twisting through the wasteland of the Judaean hills. Since the earliest times the lonely road with its hairpin bends and overhanging cliffs has been the haunt of highwaymen who found travelers easy prey and the deserted hills ideal hideaways. For centuries there has been an inn at the halfway point between Jerusalem and Jericho, and the ancient foundations and rock cisterns below the building in this picture prove that it dates from Roman times at least. Today it is an Arab police station, but if you walk through the arched entrance you will find yourself in the courtyard of the old inn. This is an oriental inn, or caravanserai, a plain low building built around a court where animals can be sheltered and watered at night.

It was this inn that figured in Jesus' parable about the Good Samaritan. The Samaritans were a Jewish sect, but there was a fierce antagonism between them and the Israelites of the parent religion. In Christ's time the Samaritans were a despised people, and other Jews would have no dealings with them. When Jesus preached that one should love one's neighbor, He was asked, "Who is my neighbor?" for in rabbinical law a Jew's neighbor could only be a fellow Israelite. It was then that Jesus told the story of a traveler who fell among thieves on the road from Jerusalem to Jericho and was left stripped and half dead. A priest and a Levite ignored his plight but a despised Samaritan stopped to bind up the man's wounds, and took him to the inn that we see here. Jesus asked which of the three was a neighbor to the unfortunate traveler, and His questioner was forced to admit, "He that showed mercy on him." "Go, and do thou likewise," was Jesus' admonishment. This unpretentious little building takes on a special luster as a result of that story, and "good Samaritan" has come to be a compliment paid to anyone of a generous and helpful nature.

SAMARITANS AT NABLUS: VANISHING SECT

THERE are only about 300 Samaritans left in the world today, and they live in the Arab town of Nablus (NAB-*luhs*) in that section of the Holy Land that once was known as Samaria. Their religion is very much like the Judaism from which it sprang, but the Samaritans believe that the center of their worship should be on Mt. Gerizim (GEHR-*ih-zim*), behind Nablus, while the Jews consider Jerusalem their holy city. And the Samaritans accept only the first five books of the Old Testament as Scripture, regarding all the later writings—Psalms, Prophets, Chronicles, Kings, Judges—as not divinely inspired.

In this picture the bearded patriarchs are displaying their ancient scroll of the Pentateuch (PEN-*tuh-took*)—the first five books of the Bible. The most treasured possession of the sect is this celebrated Samaritan scroll which is supposed to have been written on lambskin by the great-grandson of Aaron. The Samaritans' most important holiday is the Passover, which they observe just as it was observed in Old Testament times. The 300 people leave Nablus to camp out on the top of Mt. Gerizim. In their tents on the mountaintop, under the leadership of their priests, this ancient sect resembles the Children of Israel on their flight from Egypt. The old prayers are intoned, the sacrificial lambs are slaughtered, and the ritual of ancient Israel is performed as it was more than three thousand years ago.

The Passover is celebrated with Oriental splendor by this Jewish family from distant Asia.

ON THE SHORES OF GALILEE: MOUNT OF THE BEATITUDES

THE landscape of Galilee has a serene beauty that sets it apart from the harsh hills and sun-baked colors of the rest of the Holy Land. On the shores of this northern lake, Jesus preached during the years of His ministry, and many of His words reflect the Galilee of those times. In Jesus' day the Sea of Galilee was ringed with cities, and military roads from the north met caravan routes from the east, imparting an international flavor to this lively trade center.

The blue waters of this lovely lake have always harbored an abundance of fish of many species, and fishermen today cast their nets from little boats just as Peter, Andrew, James and John used to do, pulling in a silvery catch of great variety. "The kingdom of heaven is like unto a net, that was cast into the sea, and gathered of every kind," said Jesus. And choosing some of His disciples from among the fishermen of Galilee, He told them, "Follow me, and I will make you fishers of men."

Jesus traveled all about Galilee, preaching and healing, and His fame spread far beyond it. At last, followed by great multitudes of people, Jesus came to the hill in this picture. We can imagine its slope thronged with persons of every kind, and faces from many lands turned up towards Jesus. A breeze from the Sea of Galilee may have been blowing then as it does now, while herons, cranes and waterfowl splashed near the shore below and flapped through the air. The fields were ablaze with spring wildflowers, and it was against this background that the Sermon on the Mount was delivered. Near the end of the Sermon, when Jesus said, "Behold the fowls of the air: for they sow not, neither do they reap . . ." and "Consider the lilies of the field . . . they toil not, neither do they spin," He must have been drawing the examples from this peaceful landscape. A gray and white chapel crowns the Mount of the Beatitudes now and Franciscan Sisters welcome pilgrims to the tranquil shrine.

VILLAGE OF BETHANY: ST. LAZARUS CHURCH

THREE miles from Jerusalem, on the eastern slope of the Mount of Olives, lies Bethany, the little town that Jesus delighted to visit. Nowadays it is an Arab village of about 800 persons whose stone houses are scattered like ruins on the rocky hill. But nineteen hundred years ago Bethany must have been a pleasant town, for the Gospels tell us that Jesus used to stay here when He went to Jerusalem for the Passover holidays and He would return to Bethany each evening rather than remain overnight in the proud capital city.

Jesus' friends, Mary, Martha and their brother Lazarus, lived in Bethany, and it was here that Christ performed one of His most dramatic miracles. It had become dangerous for Jesus to be in Judaea, but when Mary and Martha sent for Him because their brother was sick, Jesus journeyed to Bethany to help. By the time He arrived, Lazarus had been dead for four days. Standing at the grave and weeping for His friend, Christ demanded that the stone be removed from the entrance of the burial cave. Then He cried with a loud voice, "Lazarus come forth." Lazarus appeared, wrapped in his shroud, and when news of his resurrection spread throughout the countryside people thronged to Bethany to see the man and his Saviour. It was from Bethany that Jesus rode in triumph to Jerusalem for the holiday, followed by crowds of believers, and greeted by still others bearing palm branches.

The gleaming white church in this picture was built by American Franciscans in recent years, and it stands on the traditional site of Lazarus' house where Jesus had been a frequent guest. Near the church, set in the wall of ancient rocks that we see here, is the tomb of Lazarus. Two villagers have paused to pass the time of day at the spot where Jesus announced, "I am the resurrection and the life." In the Holy Land the trivialities of everyday life take place today where events of great moment once occurred.

DAMASCUS GATE: ENTRANCE TO JERUSALEM

JERUSALEM is a city divided, with the old town belonging to Jordan, while Mt. Zion and the sprawling new suburbs to the south and west are owned by Israel. Old Jerusalem, standing high on its hills, is surrounded with crenelated walls of golden stone built by a Turkish sultan in the sixteenth century. In this picture we are just inside the walls, facing the Damascus Gate, the northern entrance to the city. The great highway from the north coming from Damascus through Nazareth and Nablus leads to this gate, and here the Three Wise Men may have tethered their camels while they went to Herod's palace to inquire about the newborn Child whose star they had seen in the East.

Camels and donkeys still pick their way through the narrow medieval streets of the town, laden with goods. The streets climb steeply, and some of them are mere alleys or flights of steps squeezed between ancient stone buildings. No cars can be driven through Old Jerusalem, but a stream of fascinating pedestrians flows through the streets. You can see Bedouin women with tattooed faces, Arab porters stooping beneath unbelievably heavy burdens, water carriers with full goatskin containers, turbaned merchants, bearded priests in flowing black robes and Arab police and Legionnaires in khaki. For the Holy City is an armed frontier, and if you look carefully you will see sandbags and soldiers neatly camouflaged on the tawny ramparts of Jerusalem.

In a bazaar in Old Jerusalem the ancient cobbled street is sheltered by an arched Crusader roof.

GIANT CANDELABRUM: ISRAELI JERUSALEM

ONCE again Jerusalem is a capital. Here in the oldest capital city of the world the new nation of Israel has established the seat of its government. The Knesset (*k'ness*-SET), or parliament, stands at the very heart of modern Jerusalem, and in the Knesset Garden we see this giant candelabrum which was a gift of the British parliament. The traditional seven-branched Menorah (*muh*-NO-*rah*) is the holy candelabrum of the Jewish temple, and its branches symbolize the seven days of creation and the seven planets (all that were known in ancient times).

Standing before the Menorah is one of the pious citizens of Jerusalem whose flowing beard and long uncut sidecurls show that he has complied with the Biblical injunction, "Neither shalt thou mar the corners of thy beard." The people of Jerusalem have gathered from nearly every country of the world, and there are now nearly two hundred thousand of them as compared with eighty-four thousand in 1949. The Law of Return, the very first law passed by this nation on its first day of existence, said that Israel's doors were to be open to any Jew, and citizenship would be granted automatically. While Israel is a vigorous modern country whose citizens are engaged in building a brave new nation, the Holy City of Jerusalem is the place that has been mystically enshrined in the hearts of the pious. Their watchword has long been the psalmist's cry, "If I forget thee, O Jerusalem, let my right hand forget its cunning." Thousands have remembered and returned.

The Wailing Wall, the last remnant of their great Temple, is no longer accessible to Jews who offered up their mournful prayers here.

שמע
ישראל

CHURCH OF THE HOLY SEPULCHER: VIEW FROM THE BELL TOWER

WITHIN the walls of Old Jerusalem, on the site of Calvary and the Tomb of Jesus, stands the Church of the Holy Sepulcher. The earliest Christians revered the place where the Cross had stood and the nearby Tomb where Christ was buried. But the Roman Emperor Hadrian, in an attempt to stamp out all memories of sacred sites, built pagan temples over the revered places of the Holy Land. Not until the fourth century, when Christianity became an accepted religion, did the first Church of the Holy Sepulcher rise here.

In 1099, when the army of the Crusades stormed into Jerusalem under the banner of Godfrey of Bouillon (*boo*-YAWNG), the Crusader Kingdom of Jerusalem came into being. His followers wanted to make Godfrey the first king, but he refused, saying, "God forbid that I should wear a crown of gold where my Master wore a crown of thorns." The Church of the Holy Sepulcher was in a sad state, and the Crusaders set about rebuilding it. The present structure is in large part the grand and noble church of the Crusaders with some later additions. Today ownership of the Holy Sepulcher is divided among a number of sects and since it is difficult to get the Eastern Orthodox, Roman, Coptic, Syrian, Armenian and Abyssinian groups to agree about the needed repairs, the church grows increasingly dilapidated. During the Easter holidays both the narrow Via Dolorosa (VEE-*yah doh-loh*-ROH-*sah*) leading to the church and the chapels inside it are brilliant with the magnificent robes of the Eastern priests, each group with its own ritual and its separate chapel, though all share the Rotunda of the Holy Sepulcher.

From the bell tower high over Jerusalem, the Holy City seems bathed in a serene light. The Cross rises above one building, while beyond it the Crescent of Islam crowns the Dome of the Rock where Solomon's Temple stood. Its altar rock, on which Abraham prepared to sacrifice Isaac, is venerated by Moslems who believe that the Prophet Mohammed ascended to heaven from it, leaving his footprint in the stone.

THE DOME OF THE ROCK: MOSLEM SANCTUARY

THE Temple area where the Dome of the Rock stands has been holy ground for at least three thousand years. A succession of sacred buildings—Jewish, Roman, Christian and finally Moslem—have been raised above the Rock of Moriah (*moh*-RYE-*uh*), where Abraham was told to offer up his son. It was here, too, that Jesus drove out the moneychangers and the people who sold sacrificial animals on the Temple grounds.

Now this area is dominated by the mosque we see in this picture. Built in the seventh century, it is one of the glories of Eastern architecture with its walls of glazed tile surmounted by a melon-shaped dome. Most of Old Jerusalem's eighty thousand citizens are Moslems, and tradition says that the scales of Judgment Day will hang from this graceful arcade to weigh their good and evil deeds.

The decorations on this pilgrim's house include blue handprints—a superstitious symbol for warding off evil.

The Dome of the Rock is one of the chief Moslem shrines, but still it is the obligation of all true believers of Islam to make a pilgrimage to Mecca at least once in their lifetime. When they return from their journey, the pilgrims paint their house fronts white and decorate them with colorful designs and quotations from the Koran. A man who has traveled to Mecca bears the honorary title of Hadji (HAH-*djee*) from that time forth, and he knows that his pilgrimage will help balance the Judgment Day scales in his favor.

GARDEN OF GETHSEMANE: ANCIENT OLIVE TREE

OUTSIDE the eastern wall of Jerusalem the land drops down into a stony valley, then rises again to the Mount of Olives. Near the foot of the hill a garden blooms, its bright flowers and cool shade a blessed relief from the searing brightness all around it. Eight gnarled olive trees still spread their branches above the flowers, and the drone of bees and the shrill whirring of grasshoppers are the only sounds heard. This is the Garden of Gethsemane, where Jesus came with the disciples the night before the Crucifixion. It was here under the olive trees that He flung Himself to the ground and prayed, "O my Father, if it be possible, let this cup pass from me: nevertheless not as I will, but as Thou wilt." And in this garden, bright with moonlight, Judas betrayed Jesus to the party of soldiers who sought Him.

Franciscan monks have lovingly tended Gethsemane for the past three hundred years. Of all the sects in the Holy Land, they wear the plainest habits—coarse brown cloth tied with the rope of St. Francis, knotted three times to remind them of their vows of poverty, chastity and obedience. The Franciscans have been caretakers of the Holy Places for the Western church since the Crusades, and they have beautified as well as preserved them. In this memorable garden the ancient trees still bear fruit and the friars press oil from their olives. In Jesus' time oil from the olives of Gethsemane was used for the Temple lamps. Today the olive pits are as precious as the oil, for the Franciscans make them into rosaries for the head of their order, the Father Custodian of the Holy Land. No one knows how old these trees are, but they were ancient at the time of the Moslem conquest. The awesome possibility exists that their twisted branches sheltered Christ in His Agony.

HOLY LAND WOMEN: ETERNAL LANDSCAPE

A DUSTY road runs past Jerusalem's eastern wall. On one side the city rises above it in golden majesty, on the other lies the Kidron (KID-*run*) Valley and the lower slopes of the Mount of Olives and Gethsemane. Thousands of ancient tombs are scattered over the rocky ground and it is here that the Jews and Moslems believe the resurrection will take place and the call to the Last Judgment will sound. There is almost no landscape in the Holy Land that does not have some Biblical significance, and this little rock-strewn vale is the place that Joel prophesied would be the "valley of decision."

History has ebbed and flowed over this land, and the centuries have brought their changes. The last two decades in particular have carried much of the modern world to the ancient country. Yet, when we look at these two women in their brilliant robes and at the sun-bleached scene behind them, we know we are seeing the world as it was in the time of the Bible. A visit to those places in the Holy Land that are timeless and unchanging takes us out of the twentieth century and back to the days when great faiths were born here. In an age of material and scientific progress it is good to turn for a while to the source of our spiritual achievements, and we find it in the eternal Holy Land.

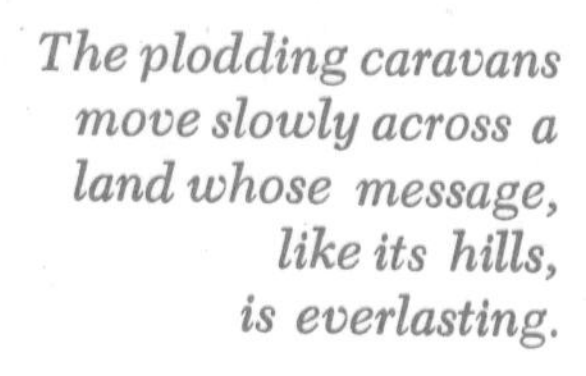

The plodding caravans move slowly across a land whose message, like its hills, is everlasting.

SOME IMPORTANT DATES IN HOLY LAND HISTORY

c. 5000 B.C.	*Jericho a flourishing city.*
c. 2000-1700 B.C.	*Time of Abraham. Journey of tribe from Mesopotamia to Palestine.*
c. 1700-1300 B.C.	*Israelites enter Land of Goshen in Egypt.*
c. 1350 B.C.	*Moses leads Israelite exodus from Egypt into Canaan.*
c. 1250-1200 B.C.	*Israelites under Joshua conquer Palestinian city-states.*
c. 1175 B.C.	*Philistines sail from Greek islands to coast of Palestine.*
1020-922 B.C.	*Israelites settle on both banks of Jordan River. Monarchy of Saul (c. 1020 B.C.), David (1013-961 B.C.) and Solomon (961-922 B.C.)*
745-732 B.C.	*Assyrians conquer Palestine.*
587 B.C.	*Beginning of Babylonian captivity of the Jews. Fall of Jerusalem.*
539 B.C.	*Cyrus II of Persia conquers Babylonia, restores Judah. Many Jews return, rebuild Solomon's Temple (515 B.C.).*
330 B.C.	*Alexander the Great conquers Phoenicia, controls Palestine.*
323 B.C.	*Death of Alexander. Palestine falls to Ptolemy, founder of dynasty which rules Egypt for 300 years.*
200 B.C.	*Seleucus I of Syria defeats Ptolemies, controls Palestine.*
167 B.C.	*Judas Maccabeus leads Israelites in revolt against Syrian king.*
63 B.C.	*Pompey the Great takes over Greek empire. Reorganizes Palestine under Roman rule with Jewish priest-kings.*
c. 5 B.C.	*Jesus born in Bethlehem.*
c. 26 A.D.	*Beginning of Jesus' ministry.*
c. 30 A.D.	*Jesus crucified in Jerusalem.*
71	*Romans destroy Jerusalem, exile the Jews and rename the country Palestine.*
395	*Palestine becomes part of Byzantine Empire.*
636	*Byzantine territory in Syria and Palestine falls to Arabs under Omar.*
1096-1291	*Period of Crusades. Kingdom of Jerusalem.*
1291-1516	*Mameluke sultans of Egypt rule Palestine.*
1400	*Mongolians under Tamerlane devastate Holy Land.*
1516	*Ottoman Turks defeat Mamelukes. Rule Palestine until 1918.*
1918	*Turks defeated by British in World War I. Palestine governed under British mandate.*
1946	*Transjordan obtains independence.*
1947	*United Nations proposal for partition followed by Jewish-Arab guerrilla warfare in Palestine.*
May 14, 1948	*Proclamation of the state of Israel. Arab League launches armed attack against her.*
Feb. 1949	*Armistice agreements signed by Israel, Egypt, Jordan, Lebanon and Syria, with battle lines setting new borders.*

SOME FAMOUS NAMES IN HOLY LAND HISTORY

Jesus of Nazareth, Mary, Joseph and various other holy figures of the Christian faith appear in the text but are not listed separately here.

ABRAHAM (c. 2000 B.C.)—*Old Testament Patriarch who brought his family into Canaan and made first covenant with God. Father of Isaac; grandfather of Jacob.*

MOSES (c. 1300 B.C.)—*Israelites' great spiritual leader; led them from Egypt. Brought the Ten Commandments and laws of God.*

JOSHUA (c. 1250 B.C.)—*Led Israelites in invasion and settlement of Canaan. Conquered Jericho.*

DAVID (c. 1013-961 B.C.)—*One of greatest figures in Hebrew history and literature. United and strengthened nation. Built capital city of Jerusalem. Many psalms attributed to him.*

SOLOMON (c. 961-922 B.C.)—*Enterprising Israelite king famous for his wisdom and the splendor of his court. Erected the Temple at Jerusalem.*

HIRAM (c. 989-936 B.C.)—*King of Tyre (970-936 B.C.); friend and ally of Solomon. Helped build Solomon's Temple.*

ALEXANDER THE GREAT (c. 356-323 B.C.)—*Conquered most of Palestine in 332. Brought Greek culture and language to the East. Old Testament translated into Greek, New Testament written in Greek.*

HEROD THE GREAT (c. 73 B.C.-4 B.C.)—*King of Judaea (c. 39 B.C.-4 B.C.). Converted to Judaism. Built city of Caesarea. Began rebuilding Great Temple at Jerusalem.*

AUGUSTUS CAESAR (27 B.C.-14 A.D.)—*Ruled Roman Empire, including Holy Land, during Jesus' ministry.*

HEROD ANTIPAS (4 B.C.-34 A.D.)—*Ruler of Galilee at time of Christ's death. Put John the Baptist to death.*

PONTIUS PILATE (22 B.C.-36 A.D.)—*Procurator of Judaea under Emperor Tiberius. Tried and condemned Jesus Christ.*

MOHAMMED (c. 570-632)—*Arabian prophet and founder of Mohammedan religion. Author of the Koran, the Islamic scripture.*

OMAR I (c. 581-644)—*Moslem conqueror of Jerusalem (638). Decreed that sacred rock of the Temple was site of Mohammed's ascension to heaven, and henceforth a Moslem shrine.*

GODFREY OF BOUILLON (c. 1061-1100)—*French Crusader. Led successful assault on Jerusalem (1099). First ruler of Kingdom of Jerusalem.*

SALADIN (1138-1193)—*Sultan of Egypt and Syria; campaigned to drive Christians from Palestine and defeated them in 1187.*

RICHARD THE LIONHEARTED (1157-1197)—*King of England. Started Third Crusade (1189). Conquered Cyprus, aided in capture of Acre, recaptured Jaffa from Saladin.*

SULEIMAN I THE MAGNIFICENT (c. 1496-1566)—*Turkish Sultan. Built Damascus Gate and restored walls of Jerusalem.*

EDMUND H. H. ALLENBY (1861-1936)—*British General, later Field Marshal. Defeated Turks at Megiddo (Armageddon). In 1917 entered Old City of Jerusalem; first Christian conqueror since Middle Ages.*

CHAIM WEIZMANN (1874-1952)—*Chemist, scholar, first President of Israel. Secured Balfour Declaration (1917) in favor of Jewish national home in Palestine as result of his successful work on explosives for British in World War I.*

DAVID BEN-GURION (1886-)—*Prime Minister of Israel (1949-1963). Served in Allenby's campaign against Turks.*

KING HUSSEIN (1935-)—*King of Jordan; acceded to throne in August, 1952.*

LEVI ESHKOL (1895-)—*Prime Minister of Israel.*

SOME HEBREW AND ARABIC WORDS AND PHRASES

Here is a list of words and phrases in the Hebrew and Arabic languages which would be useful to know when traveling in the Holy Land. The words are written in simple phonetics with the accented syllable in small capitals.

	Hebrew	Arabic
Do you speak English?	*hah-m'dah-*BEHR *ah-*TAH *ahn-*GLEET?	B'TEH-*kee in'*GLEE-*see*?
What do you want?	*mah ah-*TAH *roh-*TSEH?	*shoo bee-*TRID?
How do you say . . . ?	*eh ah-*TAH *oh-*MEHR . . . ?	*kif bit ool . . . ?*
Where is (are) . . . ?	*eh-*FOH . . . ?	*wen . . . ?*
How far?	*kah-*MAH *rah-*HOHK?	*addesh dah-*YEED?
Come here.	BOH-*oo* HEH-*nah.*	*tahl hohn.*
Please.	*b'vah-kah-*SHAH.	*min* FADD-*lahk.*
Pardon.	*s'lee-*HAH.	*al* AH-*foo.*
Thank you.	*toh-*DAH.	*shoo-*KRAHN.
Hello . . . . Goodbye (Peace).	*shah-*LOHM.	*sah-*LAHM. *mah-ess-sah-*LAHM.
water	*mah-*YEEM	MAH-*ee*
breakfast	*ah-roo-*HAHT *boh-*KERR	*ter-*WEE-*ah*
dinner	*ah-roo-*HAHT EH-*rehv*	AH-*shah*
men's room	*g'vah-*REEM	} *beht-al-*MAH-*ee*
ladies' room	*g'vah-*ROHT	
automobile (taxi)	OH-*toh* (*moh-*NEET)	*al taxi*
bus	OH-*toh-bus*	*al boos*
airplane	*ah-vee-*ROHN	*al tah-yah-rah*
baggage	*hah-vee-*LOHT	*al ag-*GRAHB
hotel	*beht mah-*LOHN	*al hotel*

DAYS OF THE WEEK

Sunday	*yohm ree-*SHOHN	*al ah-had*
Monday	*yohm sheh-*NEE	*al iz-mane*
Tuesday	*yohm shlee-*SHEE	*al sah-lah-*SAH
Wednesday	*yohm r'vee-*EE	*al err-*BAH-*ah*
Thursday	*yohm hah-mee-*SHEE	*al ham-*MEES
Friday	*yohm shee-*SHEE	*al* JOO-*mah-ah*
Saturday	*shah-*BAHT	*al sahbt*

NUMBERS

one	*eh-*HAHD	WAH-*ed*
two	*sh-*NAH-*yeem*	*t'nane*
three	*shloh-*SHAH	TLAH-*tee*
four	*ahr-bah-*AH	AR-*bah-ah*
five	*hah-mee-*SHAH	HAHM-*see*
six	*shee-*SHAH	*sitt-ee*
seven	*shee-*VAH	SAH-*bah-ah*
eight	*shmoh-*NAH	T'MAH-*nee*
nine	*tee-*SHAH	TISS-*ah-ah*
ten	*ah-sah-*RAH	AAH-*shah-rah*
one hundred	*meh-*AH	MEE-*yeh*
one thousand	EH-*leff*	*alf*

MONEY

Israeli pound	*lee-*RAH
Agorot (100 equal 1 pound)	*ah-goh-*ROHT
Jordanian dinar	*dee-*NAHR
fils (1000 equal 1 dinar)	*fills*

INDEX